PAIN FREE GOLF
© 2010 Fred Brattain

All Rights Reserved

Pain Free Golf

If you love golf but have had to play less, or give up the game because it hurts to play, this book is for you. We can show you how to play without strain on your back, and without strain on any of your other joints. How can we make this promise? Simple, I am a disabled vet with 3 ruptured disks in my lower back, two in my neck and a veteran of 13 knee surgeries. I cannot play without knee braces, and watching me trying to be graceful is NOT a pretty sight. However, I can play 36 holes a day pain free and comfortably maintain a 4 handicap with a minimum of practice.

What I have learned about the golf swing and how it really works is contained in this book. Will you be able to read this book and immediately do what I do? NO, of course not. It takes at least 90 days of practice to start cementing physical habits. Nothing physical is learned without correct practice. If you don't do the drills exactly as outlined, you will not learn what is here. There is NO shortcut to good golf, and there is NO shortcut to pain free golf.

You must do the drills correctly and regularly to learn what you need to know.

What I can guarantee is that none of these drills, when done correctly will ever hurt your back or knees or hips or neck. But you MUST practice.

Golf magazines make a fortune each year by selling the latest and greatest tips to a ravenous public who wish to find the holy grail of the golf swing in one easy $\frac{1}{2}$ page article. IT DOESN'T WORK THAT WAY!

The golf swing is a simple movement when performed in conformance with the laws of physics. It is a VERY complex movement when it is performed in opposition to the laws of physics. The former is a Lever Power Golf Swing (LPGS), the latter is a traditional golf swing (TGS).

How can I make this claim? What is the reasoning behind this? Here are some questions for you to answer before we move forward.

1) Why has the average score for men and women in this country not changed in over 80 years? In spite of the change from hickory to steel to graphite shafts, a MUCH better golf ball, better manufacturing techniques guaranteeing a more consistent product, space age metals in fairway clubs and drivers, the advent of the hybrids, etc., the average score has not gone down.

2) Why has the average score on the professional tours (PGA and LPGA) not gone down in 50 years?
3) Can you name a professional tour pro either male of female who is over 35 and doesn't have back trouble?
4) How come no one has ever broken Byron Nelson's scoring average record for 1945? There are better balls, better equipment and better conditioned players. Yet no one has come close to breaking his record. Why?

The answer is very simple. The golf swing as traditionally taught does not have physics in its favor, but rather requires exceptional timing which even the professionals cannot accomplish on a regular basis.

The Lever Power Golf Swing, as invented by Jack Kuykendall (my teacher) uses physics to the advantage of the player, instead, and requires no magical sense of timing to accomplish.

If you follow through with your desire to play pain free and learn what is in the pages of this book, and study the PowerPoint Presentation that can be ordered from my website www.disabilitygolfer.com you will hit the ball farther, straighter and pain free.

IF however, you decide that you can take PART of what we are showing you here and use it without learning the entire system, you will fail, probably hurt yourself and continue to wallow in mediocrity and pain. This is not a book of golf tips. It is a SYSTEM that will allow you to play pain free.

Were I able to be there with you on this journey, my job as your instructor would be to find the images that work the best for you. Therefore there will be a bunch of places where I talk about how the golf swing feels. Even the great Ben Hogan who was known to practice for hours and hours every day said "I play by feel." We all do.

READY?
Let's Go!!!

Traditional Golf
vs.
Lever Power Golf

Throughout this book we will be dispelling myths that are perpetrated by the traditionalists in golf. Do not misunderstand, I love and honor golf's traditions in every way except the golf swing. ☺. As one very wise person said, "The way the golf swing is taught is a religion, not a science". We are going to take a sound, scientific approach based on the Newtonian Laws of Physics, and the basics of physiology and kinesiology.

Remember, the primary postulate of scientific research is this: If a repeatable set of events does not conform to the current model/explanation of a phenomenon (the golf swing), then THE CURRENT MODEL/EXPLANATION IS WRONG!

Myth #1 – The legs provide power in a golf swing. WRONG. If this were true, the long hitters on professional tours would not be able to hit the ball just as far kneeling as they do standing up. If this were true, Chuck Hite (The Hit Man) would not be able to hit a golf ball over 300 yards STANDING ON A BASKETBALL.

Mr. Hite demonstrated this for several of the top rated teachers in the nation, and they all came away shaking their heads and saying what he did was impossible. Of course it wasn't impossible, they just saw it. But instead of realizing and accepting that their theories as to the engine in a golf swing were wrong and learning, they simply said "That didn't happen" and went on their way continuing to preach what they believe in spite of the evidence to the contrary.

TRUTH #1 – no power comes from the legs. They merely provide a stable base from which to swing your arms. If you are in a wheelchair and cannot stand, there are carts available that allow you to have a stable base from which to swing your arms. More about that later.

MYTH #2 – The hands should be passive during the golf swing. WRONG. The hands are the connection between you and the golf club.

TRUTH #2 – rotating the forearms, also called releasing the club head, is a motion that comes from aggressive use of the hands and provides over 60% of the power in a golf swing.

MYTH #3 – It is necessary to "clear your hips" and turn violently out from under the ball in order to hit the ball well. A corollary to this is the false belief that slicing the ball comes from not turning your hips out of the way.

TRUTH #3 – turning your hips, or "clearing" is necessary because the grip taught in traditional instruction guarantees that you will hook the ball into the next zip code if you do NOT turn your hips.

The violent motion of attempting to turn the lower body, and the driving of the legs through the golf shot are the number one causes for pain in a golf swing.

HOOK GRIP – SLICE MECHANICS – no wonder it hurts so much and is impossible to time properly on a regular basis.

MYTH #4 –If you are right handed, golf is a left sided game, and vice versa for a left handed player. NOT TRUE.

TRUTH #4 – Your dominant hand is your trailing hand. This is the place where power originates. The role of the leading hand is to hang on; the role of the trailing (dominant) hand is to provide both power and finesse. The number of fast twitch muscles in your triceps of your dominant arm will determine how much club head speed you can develop.

One of the things that you can do to increase your clubhead speed is to buy a speed fan and swing it with an LPG swing in 3 sets of 15 swings every other day. This will help develop the muscles you need to maximize your distance. The speed fan is a golf club grip on the end of a short shaft with four big plastic vanes on it. They are available, typically for around $45.00 from a variety of golf outlets.

The other question that we get all the time because I play a set of clubs designed by my instructor which are all hybrids down through my wedges is this. "Do I need special clubs to use the LPG swing?" The answer is NO, you do not need special clubs.

I would strongly recommend that you get the oversize grips that I use. They are available by emailing me at fred@disabilitygolfer.com for $8.00 each. The oversize grips make the single axis grip much easier to adjust to, and they are significantly easier on your hands than any other grip on the market. They can be installed on any standard golf clubs by any competent club technician. If you have experience regripping your clubs, then you will have no trouble putting these grips on your clubs. Do NOT fall into the myth that bigger grips make you slice. On the contrary, as we are working with hands and arms as the only available power source for your golf swing, bigger grips make it easier to control the club head, not more difficult.

THE BIG FOUR

No, the Big Four are not Palmer, Nicklaus, Player and Trevino ☺. They are the four fundamentals of a golf swing. If you get them right, your chances of hitting a good, if not great, golf shot are almost 90%.

What we are going to show you is a NEUTRAL Grip and NEUTRAL Mechanics rather than the hook grip and slice mechanics of the traditional golf swing (TGS).

The four fundamentals are:
GRIP – how you hold the club is critical to your success.

POSTURE – How you stand, where your weight is, and your balance are critical.

STANCE – How you are oriented to the ball, ball placement, feet and shoulders, and hands, etc.

ALIGNMENT – Most people have no clue how to line up for a straight shot. This is really simple if you do it right, and requires some trust on your part at first.

We will tackle The Big Four in order.

GRIP – As we said previously the TGS grip sets your leading hand on top of the club, and your trailing hand interwoven in some way and also slightly on top of the club. Unfortunately this really doesn't work because, as you swing, your leading hand will return to a neutral position as it passes your body center.

Try the following in front of a mirror. Stand in a golf stance facing the mirror and extend the fingers of your leading hand straight from your wrist. Now, with your arm in front of you as though touching a golf club take your leading hand and put it behind you as though you are at the top of your backswing. Now, bring your hand back around your body violently as though you were swinging a club and stop when your hand is even with your body center. This is just like back hand slapping something with the back of your leading hand. Notice how the back of your leading hand is at right angles to your body and the back of your hand is SQUARE to your target line. It isn't rolled clockwise and pointing somewhere up in the air.

So when you take your leading hand grip, you need to make sure that the back of your leading hand is parallel with the leading edge of the clubface. The clubface angle at impact is going to be the "neutral position" of the left hand. The only exception to this grip is chipping which we will discuss much later in the book. The role of the leading hand is to HANG ON.

The trailing hand, as we have said before provides both power and finesse. 25% of all the nerve endings in your body above the waist are in your dominant hand, specifically in the palm of that hand. Rather than placing the handle of the club in the base of your fingers we are going to place the handle of the club in the palm of the dominant/trailing hand. This is called a Single Axis Grip. It is called a single axis grip because the shaft and grip of the club will be in line with the forearm of the trailing hand. From a physics viewpoint this is the most advantageous way to strike a golf ball. Nothing else comes close to providing the advantages that a single axis grip can provide.

Study the pictures carefully. When taking your grip first hold the club with your trailing hand halfway up the shaft, holding the club at approximately 45 degrees. Place your leading hand on the club so that you have the club in the base of your fingers (this is just like a traditional grip). Close your hand around the club. You can test that the grip of the leading hand is correct by removing all your fingers from the club except for your index finger. The club should simply sit in your hand, with the butt of the club against the fleshy pad at the back of your palm.

Figure 1 - Testing your leading hand grip

Close your hand around the club.

Figure 2 - The completed leading hand grip

19

Shut the clubface 90 degrees by rotating your forearm. That is CCW for right handed players and CW for left handed players. Now extend your trailing hand and place the lifeline of your trailing hand on top of the shaft. Leaving your life line there, close your fingers around the grip. DO NOT let the trailing hand turn, simply close your fingers.

Figure 3 - Placing your trailing hand on the club

There will be a gap between the base of your little finger and the grip. This is correct.

Figure 4- The gap in the trailing hand grip

Now, rotate the club face back to square, allowing your trailing elbow to relax and collapse into your side.

Figure 5 - Setup Front View

If you have done this correctly, when your clubface is once more square to the target line, your trailing shoulder will be lower than your leading shoulder. This is as it should be.

Check Points:
1) Viewed from behind (down the target line), the grip should not be visible between your hands. Because this is a single axis grip, the grip is in line with the center of your trailing arm forearm.
2) There is a gap between the base of your little finger of your trailing hand and the grip, again because this is a single axis grip.
3) Your trailing hand is significantly more CW on the grip than in the TGS.
4) The back of your lead hand is parallel with the leading edge of the club.

This is a view of my right(trailing) hand viewed from in front of the ball. Note that the shaft is in line with my forearm. This is the basis of the single axis grip.

Figure 6 - The completed Single Axis Grip

POSTURE: Posture is how you stand when you are addressing the ball. This is the second step in hitting a good golf shot. This goes hand in hand with STANCE, but they are slightly different.

Most people, hear "stand upright, with your back straight and flex your knees". What happens is people then bend their knees by flexing them FORWARD over their toes. This leads to very poor posture and a real tendency to lose balance during the swing. What you should be doing is standing with your legs straight and your back straight. Bend from the hips, not the waist as though bowing stiffly, and SIT DOWN as though there were a stool under your fanny. Then simply flex your knees slightly, taking the tension out of them. Your posture should closely resemble a martial arts stance. Contrary to what you may have heard, your weight is actually slightly on your heels. You should be able to wiggle your toes in your shoes at address. You are not going to be rolling up onto your toes at impact, as you would with the TGS (traditional golf swing). If your weight shifts to your toes during the swing, you are off balance and will hit the shot either fat or thin depending on whether you stand up during the shot or not.

NOTE: When you miss a shot, most people will say "You looked up" In reality 98% of the time you STOOD up in order to keep your balance. This is a subtle difference, but easily corrected with correct posture. If you are on balance at address (correct posture) there is no need to stand up or look up to keep your balance through impact.

Now, with your club held in front of you at approximately 45 degrees, lower your arms, while standing up, and then sit further until the club contacts the ground. During this maneuver you will have to bend more from the hips for the shorter clubs. Don't make the mistake of rolling forward onto your toes, or hunching your shoulders to get closer to the ground. Both of these will result in a loss of balance during the swing.

Check Points:

1) Weight is slightly back on your heels (you can wiggle your toes)
2) Knees are slightly flexed
3) A side view looks as though you are about to sit down on a stool.

Check out the photos below.

Figure 7 - Getting Ready to take your stance

Figure 8 - Bend from the HIPS, not the waist

29

Figure 9 - Sit down to the ball

STANCE: Stance is how you stand in relation to the ball. This includes how far away from the ball you stand, whether the ball is forward or back in your stance, etc. The basic rule of thumb here is that the ball will probably be further back in your stance than it has been before. This is because you will not be turning violently through the ball, which means you will not be sliding forward at impact. After you have developed your swing, the way to determine where in your stance the ball should be is to take a practice swing which mimics the swing you want to make, and notice where your club contacts the ground. The ball position is just BEHIND that contact point on the ground.

Let's deal with a common misconception right here. When you see a professional or a good player take a divot on an iron shot, the divot starts halfway through the ball forward to in front of the ball. The ball is struck, THEN the grass is struck. This is how you generate backspin and maintain great control over your iron shots.

Note also that the feet are about as wide apart as the shoulders for all full shots. Remember your lower body supplies a stable base from which to hit golf shots. It doesn't provide any power. Having a wider stance inhibits lower body sway and turn, which translates to increased stability and less tendency to move off the ball during the swing.

The distance that you stand from the ball is another thing that will change. With the TGS, you stand much closer to the ball because you are turning away from the ball and standing up on your toes before impact. When you swing your arms, the momentum of the club head makes your arms extend to their fullest extent. In a real sense, your arms "get longer". Let's divest ourselves of

one other common teaching principle in TGS
– centrifugal force. It doesn't exist. There
is no force outward from the center of a
circle. You cannot find this in any physics
book on the planet. That is why we refer to
"momentum" and "inertia" – two things which
DO exist. There is a big difference.
However, the net effect is that your arms
will be fully extended at impact if you allow
them to be. This gives you the longest radius
circle when swinging the club, which means
maximum acceleration through the hitting
area, which translates to maximum possible
clubhead speed. Check the photos below to
understand how this works.

The best way to set up is with your arms
relaxed, and the ball positioned just off the
toe of the club. This allows for your arms to
stretch out without having to stand up on
your toes to get to the ball as you would
with the TGS. You will not have to
consciously reach for the ball, your arms and

the physics of the golf swing will take care of this for you.

Figure 10- Perfect Posture

Figure 11 - Proper setup to the ball

ALIGNMENT: Alignment is how you stand to the target line. Notice in the photo above that the target line is parallel with the stripes on the practice mat. The swing path is the heavy black line that is 10 degrees inside to outside. This is required for a straight shot. Your shoulders, hips and knees are all aligned parallel to the target line. However, this can be tricky because most people tend to line up right of the target (if you are right handed) and then pull the shot left to bring the ball back on line. If you line up correctly and look over your lead shoulder you will think you are lined up way left (right handed) or way right (left handed) of your target. This is as it should be. Parallel lines do not meet at the target.

This completes our basic discussion of The Big Four. We will be referring back to these principles during the rest of our discussion.

THE LEVER POWER GOLF SWING

The Lever Power Golf Swing (LPGS) is the simplest and most effortless and effective way to hit a golf ball consistently far and straight. There are NO shortcuts. There are no halfway measures here. This swing will NOT work if you try to use only part of what we are about to show you. It is an all or nothing proposition.

Be patient with yourself. If you are learning LPG after years of using a TGS, this will take time. 90 days of constant practice is required to absorb these lessons as quickly as possible. There is also a training kit available from Jack Kuykendall which will speed up your learning process. But the fundamental issue here is GIVE THIS A CHANCE. LPG does work and does allow you to play pain free. All you have to do is do the drills, and be patient. Give your body time to learn.

In addition, we will be talking from time to time about playing golf as opposed to hitting golf balls. They are two different games. One is called "golf" the other is called "golf swing". Here for the most part we are working on "golf swing", but the ultimate goal is to get your swing so automatic that when you are playing golf on the course you don't have to play golf swing because you can't play both at the same time. ☺

What we are going to do here is build the LPG golf swing one drill at a time. In my experience, this is the most effective way to do this. Each drill requires that you attain a level of mastery before you move on to the next. This is where your self discipline is involved. If you rush this process, you will not be successful, and you will have to come back and start over. BE PATIENT.

GETTING STARTED:

In the opening of this book we debunked the myth that the golf swing is powered by the leading arm. Rather it is powered by the trailing/dominant arm regardless of whether you are right or left handed. The first drill is designed to instill this feeling of controlling the swing with your dominant hand.

An historical note here - The notion that the golf swing for right handed people is a left handed/left sided game comes from the fact that Ben Hogan was left handed but played right handed. This notion has been further promoted by the fact that both Mike Weir and Phil Mickelson are right handed but play left handed. This is a prime example of people not understanding physics and then teaching from that ignorance. In his <u>Five Lessons</u> Book, Hogan recognized the purpose of the trailing hand when he said "I discovered that the faster I rotated my right hand the further and straighter the ball flew. I wish I had two right hands."

With a sand wedge or pitching wedge, take your single axis grip, set up to the ball, which should be slightly back of center in your stance, and remove your leading hand from the club, placing it behind your back. Now, start your one handed backswing by pulling your trailing elbow back behind you, and hit the ball. This is not about hitting it as far as you can, it is about hitting the ball as cleanly as you can. The shot should look just like a regular wedge shot, high, soft and straight.

If you are coming from a TGS, your first few shots are going to go low and left, because you are turning your lower body in an attempt to help hitting the ball. You will start hitting the ball straight ahead when you focus on **facing the ball at impact and swinging from the inside of the ball away at 10 °**. Excessive body turn will destroy your ability to hit this shot. Do NOT freeze over the ball. It is perfectly normal for your body to turn back and through as you swing your arms. But the DIFFERENCE is that your arms are controlling the swing and your shoulders are turning as a RESULT of swinging your arms, not the other way around. Check the video on our PowerPoint Presentation to see how this should look.

At the finish of your follow through, which need only be as high as your waist, the clubface should be pointed down at the ground (completely shut). This is only accomplished by rotating your right trailing hand CCW for right handed players and CW for left handed players.

The feeling here is that of swinging a long hammer. You don't hold a hammer in your fingers, you hold it in the palm of your dominant hand. If you envision a nail sticking out of the back of the ball angled so that it points forward on the 10° path we have discussed, and drive the nail with your hammer/golf club, you will have the feel we are attempting to achieve here.

When you can hit an entire bucket of range balls with just your trailing hand/arm, you are ready to proceed to the next drill. Even after you are playing with the LPG swing, the first ten balls of any practice or warm-up session should be this one-handed drill.

At the risk of sounding hopelessly repetitive, do not go on to the next drill until you can perform the first one flawlessly for an entire large bucket of balls. This is the one move that all good players have in common.

The second drill teaches you to use your hands properly in the golf swing. The hands are a source of power, and not passive, as is suggested with the TGS.

Start this drill with a wedge, but progressively work through your entire bag with this drill. This drill is done with a HALF swing. Again, we are instilling a feeling in our hands and arms, we are not trying to hit the ball as far as we can.

The rotation of the hands just after impact is a critical component of control and distance within the LPG swing. In the TGS this is called "releasing the hands", but in reality rather than a passive release, it must be an active movement of the hands. Note: learning to do this will almost make slicing impossible. In order to roll the hands over after impact, we must roll them open on the backswing.

Visualization tool: Hold your cell phone or TV remote in your dominant hand with the front face of the device facing directly away from your palm. Hold your hand as though you were holding a golf club, with the palm of your dominant hand facing down the target line. As you "take the club back" by pulling your trailing elbow back, roll your hand so that the face of the device is now pointing directly up at the sky. As you swing down and through "impact" roll your hand over so that the face of the device is pointing straight down at the ground.

This is exactly the feel that you want with your golf club. So what we are going to do is take each of your clubs and practice this motion. Make SURE you have a proper single axis grip, and that you are controlling the club with your dominant/trailing hand. This should be straightforward at this point as you have already mastered the one handed swing. For right handed players roll your hands CW (open) on the backswing and roll your hands CCW (closed) just after impact.(Left handed players do the opposite) Remember there is no need to move your body around, just let it follow your arms, but YOU MUST FACE THE BALL AT IMPACT.

At the end of your $\frac{1}{2}$ follow through in this drill, the clubface will be directly facing the ground with your arms extended down the target line.

Practice this drill at 1/2 speed and using only a half swing until you are making solid contact with every club. When you are hitting all your clubs crisply using this drill, you are ready to proceed.

Just as with the one handed drill, this should be a part of your warm up routine prior to practice or play every time you go to the range or golf course.

In the TGS, there is a requirement that you allow your wrists to cock during the backswing. In the LPG swing, you do not want your leading wrist to break down at all. The way to get the feel for this is to take the club in your leading hand and lift the club allowing your elbow to bend, placing the grip on your trailing shoulder. This requires that your elbow bends, which is exactly what we want to have happen, as this is the extra lever in LEVER POWER GOLF.

When you add your trailing hand to this exercise, you will find it very easy to raise the club until it is vertical and your hands are close to your trailing shoulder. This is as far back as necessary to complete your backswing. Practice this in front of a mirror until it feels natural. This may take some time if you are coming from the TGS, but it is the ESSENCE of this golf swing.

Because we are not only allowing but rather encouraging your leading arm to bend, we are removing the twisting torque on the lower back. No longer are you required to maintain a straight leading arm, which is a primary source of back and shoulder strain.

The entire point to the bent leading arm in the backswing is the essence of LEVER POWER GOLF. When you are trying to move something with a lever, the longer the lever you have, the easier it is to move the boulder or work the jack handle to lift the car. This is simply physics. When you keep your leading arm straight, the lever that you have to impart power to the golf ball extends from your hand to the head of the club. When you bend your leading arm, you are lengthening that lever by the length of your forearm. I won't bore you with the mathematics of this, but the net effect is significantly less effort to produce the same clubhead speed.

If you have grown up with TGS, this is going to feel really awkward at first, but will reap huge dividends in the end. The ultimate goal is to do all of this by feel, which is the same as saying you have repeated the drills enough times that doing it right feels right. When I am at the top of my backswing with the club vertical, it feels to me as though the grip of the club is plastered into the palm of my right hand. It feels as though all I have to do is drive my right hand straight down by straightening my arms and then driving it through the back of the ball like a hammer.

A hammer is a great image to use here. If you hold a hammer in the base of your fingers you will have trouble putting any power into your stroke. You hold a hammer in the palm of your dominant hand in order to drive a nail. Same with the golf club. The LPG swing should feel the same way as standing next to a post and driving a nail into the post at your knees.

This is the start of the backswing. Notice the trailing elbow being pulled back and no cocking of the wrists.

Once the club is waist high in the backswing, you only need to raise your hands to your shoulders, putting the back of the trailing hand as close to your shoulder as you can without straing.

This is a front on view of the top of the
backswing. Practice this position in the

mirror. Note the minimal turn of both hips and shoulders. They are simply following the motion of the arms. This is a completed FULL backswing. There is no need to take the club back any further than this.

Once you can consistently get to the correct position at the top of your backswing, it is time to practice the start of the downswing. This is a CRITICAL move, and the one designed to take advantage of the longer lever which exists because you have bent your leading arm at the elbow, and kept your leading wrist locked rather than cocked.

From the top of your backswing the first move is to straighten your arms DOWNWARD, not around your body. For an action video of this principle, go to www.DisabilityGolfer.com and click on "videos". As your arms straighten without turning forward, the momentum of the club head will naturally return the club head to its neutral starting position. If the ball is in the proper place in your stance, this will mean that you will meet the ball with a sharply descending blow at the maximum point of club head acceleration. If you perform this move correctly, with an initial downward motion, the only thing left to do is roll your hands over through impact to create a high and penetrating shot with every club in your bag.

Remember we are making physics our ally, not our enemy with this golf swing and allowing the physics of motion to take over is exactly what we want to have happen.

Practice this drill in a mirror, and make sure that, as you start down with your hands that you are not turning toward your target. Remember the body follows the arms and you MUST face the ball at impact.

The next drill requires a special piece of equipment. You need to go to your local store and purchase a stool. I strongly recommend that you purchase one which is adjustable, as this makes finding your comfort zone much easier. WalMart has an excellent one for about $30.00. It is the one used in the PowerPoint Presentation referenced in this book.

This drill is designed to cement in your muscle memory (really in the neurons in your brain), the idea that swinging your arms is the source of power in a golf swing. With this drill you should comfortable achieve 95% of your normal distance with each club. This will also teach you that there is no need to move your lower body except to follow your arms. This is a practice drill that should be done at least once a week even after you have become an expert in the LPG swing.

Sit on your stool at a comfortable height, play the ball back a little further than usual in your stance, and hit every club in your bag sitting on the stool. Work through the bag from wedges to driver. When you are hitting the ball straight and high and an appropriate distance, it is time to move on to the full swing.

The purpose of sitting on the stool and hitting balls is twofold. 1) this teaches you to not throw your body through the ball, as it does nothing to increase club head speed and 2) it instills the feeling of standing tall but with your weight slightly on your heels when you set up and swing.

I have been playing LPG for 10 years and have taught it for the last 5. I do this drill with a large bucket of balls every week. Once you have the basic hand and arm movements down, this is the best drill to keep your swing sharp and effortless.

Congratulations!!

Having mastered these drills you are ready to start the full swing. If you have been conscientious in doing your drills, you should have the feel of the full swing already. Stand tall, and remember that less effort translates to greater distance. Seems backwards doesn't it? But it is true.

Now here is the fun part. Put your feet completely together, heels and toes touching and hit balls using your full swing. It is best to start with slow swings and only 50% effort and work your way up to a full speed swing. This drill teaches you the value of balance and tempo. If you are falling off balance, you are swinging too hard and losing control of your body. Remember your lower body ONLY provides a solid base from which to swing your arms. When you can hit the ball straight and high and far using everything we have worked on so far, with your feet together, you are ready to spread your feet apart (about shoulder width) and take a full swing.

Each of these drills should be repeated occasionally if and when you are having trouble. They are the basis of a solid LPG swing and are not just for learning the swing for the first time.

As with everyone else, I sometimes find myself not striking the ball as solidly as I would like. The feet together drill is a great way to regain that solid and quiet lower body. I will even hit a few shots during the round with my feet much closer together than normal in order to regain the feeling of swinging my arms and letting everything else follow their lead.

ARE YOU READY TO PLAY? – probably not ☺. When you come under the stress of playing the game, especially with friends looking on and making the usual incorrect and often derogatory remarks about your new swing, it is almost certain you will revert to your old swing. Everyone goes back to what they know, even if it's wrong because there is a comfort zone there.

I strongly recommend that you do not go play until you have enough confidence in your new swing that you will stick with it through thick and thin regardless of how well you play the first time out. Once the nerves are out of the way, you will find that this really works and you hit the ball better than you have in a long time and don't hurt when you get to the 19th hole.

Remember I said this isn't an overnight cure for what ails you, it is a PROCESS, and you have to have the strength of spirit to give the process time. After all, you have stuck with this game through all of its ups and downs for a long time. Why not stick with the change of a lifetime until it works?

If you want some help with how to overcome the nerves and play the best you can even under stress, visit our website at www.SingleAxisGolf.com and order the book "*The Art of Getting Out of Your Own Way.*"

THE SHORT GAME –

The simple fact is that you will never be any better than your short game. It is the part of the game that separates all players of every level. If you can hit a driver 200 yards you can play scratch golf if your short game is up to snuff.

We have devoted an entire book to this part of the game, using LPG principles throughout. If you wish to order it, go to www.SingleAxisGolf.com and order "Golf For the Rest of Us".

Please note that all proceeds from all our books go to The Disabled Golfers Learning Foundation, Inc. If you want to know more about the Foundation please visit us at www.DisabilityGolfer.com

Thank you for purchasing this book. We hope that it has helped you in your quest to play Pain Free Golf.

For a complete video discussion of these principles, write to us and order the PowerPoint Presentation. The price is $17.50 and includes shipping and handling for the US. Foreign orders, including Canada will be slightly more.

Please feel free to ask questions of us or add your comments at Fred@disabilitygolfer.com

Thanks again for your interest in playing pain free golf. We are always standing by to answer questions and provide whatever insight we can. Remember, once again, this is a journey and a process. It won't happen overnight, but the patience and attention to detail that you bring to this will be handsomely rewarded.

Fairways and Greens,

Fred Brattain

Corona, CA
2010

Made in the USA
Middletown, DE
18 July 2023

35401384R00035